The Uppity Blind Girl Poems

by
Kathi Wolfe

THE UPPITY BLIND GIRL POEMS

Editor: Clarinda Harriss
Graphic design: Ace Kieffer
Author photo: Alexander Vasiljev
Cover art: Minás Konsolas

Stonewall/BrickHouse Books, Inc. 2015
306 Suffolk Road
Baltimore, MD 21218

Distributor: Itasca Books, Inc.

ISBN: 978-1-938144-27-1

Printed in the United States of America

Acknowledgments

Some of the poems in this chapbook originally appeared in the following journals: "Happy Hour," "A Pulp Fiction," "Blindista," "Uppity's Mother Wishes Her Daughter Happy Birthday," "Maybe Chicken Little Wasn't Paranoid After All," "Love at First Sight" and "Justine's Valentine for Her Sister Uppity" appeared in *Wordgathering*. "Uppity Writes on Tinseltown's Facebook Wall" originally appeared in *Gargoyle*. "If I Had a Magic Wand," and "Grand Central Rorschach Blot" originally appeared in *Innisfree Poetry Journal*. "If I Were a Boy," "Blind Porn," "If There is an Apocalypse," "ScentsSpeakeasy: Blogspot," "Uppity's Prayer," "That's All Folks!," "Mind's Eye," "After Hurricane Sandy," "Dining with the Green-Eyed Monster," and "Sabrina's Song for Uppity" originally appeared in *Scene4*. "Uppity Blind Girl Confesses" originally appeared in *Disability Studies Quarterly*.

With heartfelt thanks to my family, friends, editors, teachers and mentors.
For all the Uppity girls.

Freedom, Skill and Joy

A Comment by Grace Cavalieri, producer/host, "The Poet and the Poem from the Library of Congress"

Here is an excerpt from Kathi Wolfe's book. A poem titled "A Pulp Fiction" begins:

> *All those lesbians you pal around with will lead into a blind alley, her*
> *grandmother told Uppity. For the love of Sappho, Uppity thought, slipping on her silver pumps,*
> *take me there! Bring me to this dyke-infested place where*
> *sapphic ghosts kiss blindly in devil-encrusted glitz. Where forbidden fruit*
>
> *ripens...*

Uppity is the girl you want to sit with at the popular kids table in the cafeteria. She's sassy, she's smart, she's funny, she's – well, she's uppity! Uppity will have a legion of fans because she would order a U-Haul truck for her senior prom chauffeured by a tuxedo-tee-shirt driver.

Kathi Wolfe is one of America's great satirists at a time when few women humorists are writing poetry. We champion her poetic will and many of us, faithful Kathi fans, follow her columns in *The Washington Blade* to see how she transforms as she reforms.

Kathi Wolfe takes wit to a higher arc in her column in *Scene4*. But I want to talk about her alter ego "Uppity." Here we find the epicenter of memory and imagination. The inherent strength in these poems is a freeing up of taboo subjects, with intellectual arguments camouflaged as stories; and a summative bravery of writing with originality.

Only a gifted poet could take a character, situation, and plot and make such a relationship with the reader that will not be forgotten. The comfort of poetry is in the surprise and discovery of the new. Of all the tools the poet has in her bright art, none surpasses the jaunty elegance of Kathi Wolfe's "Uppity."

Here is the first part of the poem "Seeing Red:"

> *"How do you explain the color red to a blind person?" The Little Book of Big*
> *Questions.*
>
> *Forget about wheelbarrows filled with hay*
> *and cows grazing in the fields outside barns;*
>
> *they're cozy, but too bucolic*
> *to dance in the retinas of unseeing eyes.*
>
> *Don't chase after matadors with their flowing capes,*
> *fainting fans, and baiting of crazed bulls;*
>
> *this butting of horns and gory frenzy*
> *disturbs the dreams of shadowed corneas.*
>
> *Skip cherry cough drops and Valentines with doilies,*
> *such elixirs stink of Victorian parlors*
>
> *and the flu. Sip a Bloody Mary, slowly, carefully,*
> *seeking solutions to all puzzles in the tabasco,*
>
> *...*

To read the rest of this poem and be thrilled with more, just sit back, light up a beer, put up your feet and take the joyride of your life with an outrageously incorrigible uppity blind girl.

Table of Contents

Happy Hour

Seeing is a nightmare for the blind,
Uppity says, sipping a beer
at the Funhouse Pub. *I must be dreaming,*
she thinks, *a roach
is doing the breast stroke in my glass!*
The bartender's nose hairs twitch.
*Her polo shirt is Pepto-Bismol colored!
There goes my fantasy of romance.*

A woman with smoke-stained teeth
sits next to Uppity, tapping
"what pimps read" onto her iPad.
Uppity looks at the ceiling to avoid
going there.

Am I getting chubby? Uppity averts
her gaze from the bar's green, moldy walls.
*Am I going gray at 22? Would I kiss
anyone with zits? Or less than perfect abs?*

Uppity munches pistachios, swigs more beer,
and plants her gold stilettos firmly on the ground.
Seeing isn't for the faint of heart, she says,
I'm not ready for my close-up.

The Planet of the Blind

You really can hear a pin drop, Uppity told
the incense-burning old lady in apartment 3B,
who, like Sherlock Holmes thoughtfully smoking
his pipe, patiently tried to deduce
how Uppity's world was different from hers.
Mirrors are for aliens, Uppity said.
The sun tastes like red velvet cake;
your lover's voice is a cashmere cape;
a clown's smile smells of orange blossom
and ashes. You are your own shadow.

A Pulp Fiction

All those lesbians you pal around with will lead into a blind alley, her grandmother told Uppity. For the love of Sappho, Uppity thought, slipping on her silver pumps, take me there! Bring me to this dyke-infested place where sapphic ghosts kiss blindly in devil-encrusted glitz. Where forbidden fruit ripens. Let me caress the shattered stone. My cane, a dagger, will slash the heart of my ex who left me standing alone on the street after the midnight show of *Wait Until Dark*. In a blind passion, my hands will stalk the crumbling wall! Looking for requited love. Like a sightless idiot, believing it can be found.

Uppity Writes on Tinseltown's Facebook Wall

Gods of Milk Duds and Coca-Cola soaked endings,
from which sighted and unsighted emerge, blinking,
in the dark, my love life is a B picture with no
coming attractions. No *alluring* strangers,
just *safe* commuters on this train. When I woo
Grace Kelly, the lady vanishes. The gum
on the floor of your cineplexes sticks
to the soles of my ruby slippers.

Gods of pop-eyed paparazzi and strobe-lit carpet,
let me eat the Danish Audrey Hepburn wouldn't touch,
don the dress Kate Hepburn wouldn't wear,
dine with the company Garbo wouldn't keep,
sing Garland to sleep during the restless night.
Let me be Frankie, dancing with Annette
on a beach blanket under starlight – no bingo –
before the mothers of America, until dawn,
when sighted and unsighted emerge into the light.

If I Were a Boy,

I'd drive,
Al Pacino in *Scent of a Woman,*
into the Macho Guy sunset,

spinning
my wheels over the heavens and the earth,
stopping only to pick up girls.

The chicks,
sneaking a peek, would die to know
how I kiss with my manly eyes closed.

Screeching
past dead-man curves,
racing the devil's own,

the secret
of my blind lip-lock will remain
tethered to my man-boy bones.

ScentsSpeakeasy.com: Blogspot

Dear Editor,
You wonder how, I, sightless, can compare
a warm-blooded, full-bodied
fragrance to a Rubens or liken
a wild, disheveled beer
to Dennis Hopper biking
in a pot-filled haze.
I should take up piano-tuning, you insist.

Tin-eared scribe, your vision
blinds you. Can you see
if a beer tastes like rubies
or smells like unwashed hair?
Unhitched from eyes, I devour secrets.
Pickled mango chutney with a touch
of papaya is my latest fave.
As a scientist maps genes,
I decode aromas, divine spirits.
Yours,
Uppity.

Love at First Sight

In an elevator trapped
between the fifteenth and sixteenth
floor of her apartment building,
Sunday morning, Elizabeth, her cane
in one hand, coffee and bagels
in the other, just in from the deli,
met Sabrina and her poodle Toto.

Maybe it was Toto dancing
like a flying monkey
around Elizabeth's cane, the wind roaring
through the elevator shaft like a twister
barreling down on Kansas, Sabrina's
pomegranate scented hair, or Elizabeth's
ruby red flip-flops. Calling loudly
for help, pressing the emergency button,
needing to pee, they were headed toward Oz.

A week later, Elizabeth and Sabrina, in bed,
followed their own Yellow Brick Road,
dreaming of rainbow ballads and Wizard blues.

"Will she have red or white?"
the bartender asked Sabrina
as she and Elizabeth sat,
holding hands, at the Tin Man Pub.
"*She'll* have an Old-Fashioned,"
Elizabeth told the server.

"Elizabeth," murmured Sabrina.
"Call me Uppity," she said, "I'm the door
that won't stay closed, the spy who cracks
the code. No wicked witch will melt me
here with my sweetie in the Emerald City."

Seeing Red

"How do you explain the color red to a blind person?" The Little Book of Big Questions.

Forget about wheelbarrows filled with hay
and cows grazing in the fields outside barns;

they're cozy, but too bucolic
to dance in the retinas of unseeing eyes.

Don't chase after matadors with their flowing capes,
fainting fans, and baiting of crazed bulls;

this butting of horns and gory frenzy
disturbs the dreams of shadowed corneas.

Skip cherry cough drops and Valentines with doilies,
such elixirs stink of Victorian parlors

and the flu. Sip a Bloody Mary, slowly, carefully,
seeking solutions to all puzzles in the tabasco,

vodka, and tomato juice; eat a ripe, sweet
strawberry as if it were your last meal.

Hold her hand as if you and the love
of your life were in Times Square at the end of World War II;

then the botched irises, appetites aroused,
alight, wide-open, will see red.

Blindista

Watch me roll my sightless eyes!
Uppity decreed at fifteen when her mother
insisted, using her dragon-lady voice,
"you must wear your hair short.
Blind girls aren't princesses,
they can't take care of long golden locks."
I don't want footmen, Prince Charming
or a fairy godmother, Uppity said. *I want to inhale*
champagne, be tickled by the feathers
of a boa around my shoulders, and swim
in the silk tresses flowing down my back.

At 25, unfurling her cane, her own feather boa
prickling her, warming her, against the rough
wind of gum wrappers, manholes and stroller
wheels, Uppity stepped out onto the street.
The tempo of the cane's tapping protected
her from the icy staccato of the jaywalkers'
cold, startled stares. *I'm Fred Astaire*
dancing with my stick, putting on the Ritz,
Uppity told the god of blindness. *I'm the Braille*
Carrie Bradshaw. I'm a blindista.

Blind Porn

Imagine reading Playboy to the blind!
exclaims the anchorwoman. *Not just the articles,*
but the pictures! she says, breathlessly.

I hope it's filthy, so sordid it gives blind
porn a bad name, Uppity whispers to Sabrina,
stroking her hair, flicking the remote,
tickling her toes under the silky sheets.

They'd clicked that night
when they kissed in Washington Square Park,
until this guy, panting, leered, *I gotta take a pic*
with my phone – two blind chicks making out.

Furies in spiked heels,
the ladies aimed – a direct hit –
Damn bitches! he screamed,
Whad'ya got – radar?

We wanna get a sound bite
of your balls turning blue!
the harpies hissed, *nothing*
would give us more bliss.

Why, to the sighted,
are we creatures
from the Black Lagoon?
Uppity wondered.
They turn off the TV,
undress,
sip wine,
check their breath,
pray to the gods
of good sex
and tenderness,
just as I do now
before making love
to my lady.

Who knows?
Uppity sighed,
if this be blind porn,
play on.

Uppity's Prayer

MSNBC suspended Alec Baldwin...After a...gay slur that he made in a confrontation with reporters. The New York Times.

Cock-suckers, faggots, dykes – wounded,
cootie-infested creatures beaten down
by the raging rapids in a leech-filled river –
Bogie and Kate – gods of the African Queen,
heal their wounds with your booze
and prayers. Delouse their scales,
bandage their bloody fins, so they'll escape –
dry, unbloodied, heads unbowed.

After Hurricane Sandy

Darkness ricochets like a rifle shot –
ambushing trees, felling power lines –
startling rats.

Before, Uppity and the night
were conjoined twins:
two girls on the town ready to raise
a glass at happy hours or to throw
frozen margaritas at intruders.

Now, tapping her cane, guiding
Sabrina and Toto into her apartment,
a blacked-out maze,
Uppity and the night were no longer BFFs.

I've never been captured by the dark,
Uppity said, huddling with Sabrina,
Toto's muddy tail smacking against their boots,
*but this blackness has nearly
trapped me in its acrid arms.*

*My cane knows gutters, manholes,
flowerbeds, subways and steps.
It is unschooled in lifeless bodies,
derailed trains and the floating remains
of drowned cars.*

*Only the warmth of Sabrina's breathing
and the salt of Toto's tongue
release me from the cold clutches of the dark.*

Maybe Chicken Little Wasn't Paranoid After All

Uppity, toes dancing in her soft shoes,
fingers tapping her white cane,
knew why Chicken Little had been afraid.

She was just calling the shots,
the shots as she saw them, using
state-of-the-art technology of her time

to place her best bet on when the heavens,
seemingly as secure as the king's castle,
would fall, Uppity thought, toasting

her 21st birthday with a Bellini with two
girlfriends in a Soho bar. Intense, if neurotic,
sky-watching, spot-on detection, acute

acorn observation were the top
predictive indicators in Chicken Little's
era. But, she'd left dumb luck

out of her prognostications, Uppity saw,
just as the doctors, those oracles,
had at her birth in 1988. The oak seed,

the gods fastening the clouds to their hinges,
kept everything safe for Chicken Little. Still,
Uppity knew why Chicken Little had been afraid.

She'll never amount to anything, the doctors,
the seers of the land, told Uppity's parents
at her birth. *Never move the furniture,*

never let her walk alone, much less ride a bike.
Who knows if she'll ever learn how to eat?
they'd asked as if the sky had already fallen.

Maybe the docs were using state-of-the-art
technology of their time, Uppity thought,
sipping her cocktail, calling the shots

as they saw them for people like me.
But, they'd left dumb luck out of their
prognostications. Her father believed

in poker, her mother worshipped
Fred Astaire. If the sky did fall,
they never saw it.

Grand Central Rorschach Blot

1.
You're a hunter out for the kill,
my Dad loved to shoot deer, growls
a man with a frayed beard voice.
I'm buying a ticket to New Haven or anywhere
away from Hunter Man, who insists my white
cane is a walking stick that could really scare
the bejesus out of you if used the right way.
Wish I'd had one last night, he says, *It would*
have knocked my wife into shape.

2.
I'm sitting at the counter at the Oyster Bar,
cane collapsed, playing Radio Life.
You look like a waif held together by paperclips,
whispers a young woman smelling of lemon and garlic,
who's convinced my stick is a painter's brush.
I paint, too, she says, *drunks, trees, spaghetti,*
faces, once estranged, now intimate, chimps.
I see so many pictures in your bloodshot eyes,
marvels the New Rousseau.

3.
What's your handicap? asks a boy on the platform.
Grabbing my cane, he says, *I'm ten. Before my*
Mom left my Dad to live with Peter – this jerk
with nose hairs and crooked ears – she took me
to see Tiger Woods at the Masters. That almost
made up for their fights. I wanna be like Tiger.
Tiger Wannabe takes a ball from his pocket
and swings at it with my stick. *I bet you*
practice your swing a lot, he says.

Uppity Blind Girl Confesses

You think I'm musical,
I write opera
for the tone-deaf.
In fact, the gods
cut off their ears
when they hear me sing.

I stare back
as you gaze into my face,
mining crows feet
for some inner vision.

I do not want
to feel your face.
Believe me, I
don't live in a vale
of tears
because I can't see
your pores.

You long
to sew me up
as you'd mend
your torn Raggedy Anne doll.
But I'm my own puppet.
I pull my own strings.

Dining with the Green-Eyed Monster

I didn't invite her to dinner,
but there she was: pulling
up a velvet chair, sitting down,
munching kale chips,
sipping emerald ale.
You're spared the sight
of my verdant eyes,
the monster said,
but my jade fangs lust for you.

Who would want to tryst
with such a beast?

Still, I remembered:
the things I couldn't see
from Yellow cabs to indigo trees;
the people who denied
my Third Eye
and thrived
like downy kudzu on the vine;
the day my sister Justine
danced at her junior prom
and I missed the word *praline*
at the eighth grade spelling bee;
the night Sabrina,
after too many tequila shots,
kissed another girl.

I'll never accept your venomous caresses,
I told the monster, *but let's enjoy this feast.*

If I Had a Magic Wand,

I'd turn unwanted prayers into shout-outs
for lonely stars, neglected clouds, cats

clamoring for catnip, the boy who grabbed
my shoulder, keeping me from lurching

into the abyss below the subway platform,
Uppity told Sabrina after a woman,

smelling like burnt toast, patted her on the head,
muttering, *I'm praying for you. If you repent,*

Jesus will open your eyes and wash your sins away.
You'd see the world the Lord has made.

I've sinned with the best of them, Uppity said,
from cheating on a math test in junior high

to forgetting to feed the goldfish to stealing
my sister's boyfriend. If I had a magic wand,

I'd wash my sins away faster than the latest
Twitter trend. But my eyes don't need

to be opened. I see all too well the world
that the Lord has made. My selfie

is all too clear to me. I'm the Dalai Lama
of imperfection. Promise me, Sabrina,

if you pray for me, use your magic wand
to comfort and anoint my upturned eyes.

Uppity's Mother Wishes Her Daughter Happy Birthday
Thanksgivukkah, 2013

As I light the candle in the menorah,
we sing "dreidel, dreidel, dreidel,"
and the dog begs for bites of leftover turkey,
you, your Dad and Sabrina fight for dear
life over the last sweet potato latke.
If a bookie had taken odds,
who'd have bet that we'd ever see
such an evening – an overstuffed bird –
ready to burst with gratitude and light?

No one, twenty-five years ago, when you
burst forth on a cold winter night –
disrupting the Festival of Lights.
Then, looking into your unlit eyes,
I saw only a gray whirlwind.

A West Side Job, pacing with you
in my living room on 79th Street,
I demanded of God: *Have You no eyes?*
Can You not see what You've done?
What's in Your unholy bag of tricks
for my baby Elizabeth? Selling pencils
on the street corner? Stringing beads
like Selina in a Patch of Blue? Begging
as jaded strangers look away?
Your Festival of Lights is a boil
on the flesh of Your darkened universe.

Still, no matter how hard I tried to blindfold
myself, Elizabeth, you were a rogue laser
beaming everything within your reach. At five,
when you ate your best friend Eddy's
chocolate bears and devoured the treats
as if you were the whale swallowing Jonah,
a ray sneaked on to my field of vision.
Damned if the sun didn't shine, when in middle
school, you stole second playing softball –
a beep telling you when you reached the base.

Light leapt through the window on the day
you started your blog and told me,
Literature is my utopia, Helen Keller said.
I'm not a Helen wannabe. I'm going
to map the Twitterverse like explorers
of old named the constellations.

No wonder we call you Uppity!
A quarter century on, no one
can dim your star-studded shine.

Justine's Valentine for Her Sister Uppity

Thief, from day one, you stole
my teddy bears, chewing gum;
for more fun, you jumped
into my bubble bath, splashing
with perfect pitch radar soap
into my eyes. *You're like me
now,* you giggled when I wailed
that I couldn't see, *don't cry,
the shampoo smells like peaches.*

Brat, early on, you moved me,
a pawn, across your chessboard.
Ruled by your shadow-sister eyes,
I could see I'd never get to say
checkmate. When, Homer
in Central Park, you sang
of unicorns in tails and top hats
smoking pot on the lawn, I
couldn't resist your siren song.
I followed your cane high
up to the sky: even when you
told Mom that only I was stoned.

Witch, from time before memory,
you've bewitched with your trickery,
taken the spotlight in every room,
bewildered with your mystery.
Yet, there would be no light
if not for your dark coven.

Mind's Eye

If I were Queen of the World,
ruling with my Royal Smart Phone,
Bluetooth in tiara, walking
my besotted, blue-blood dogs,
regally motioning to my worshipful
subjects to stop curtsying,
only my bejewelled cane
would dig its way
into the tunnel of your vision.

If I won the Nobel Prize for cracking
the passwords of the dead,
only my encrypted, blinkered eyes
would register in your retinas.

If Sabrina and I were making love,
nymphs on the loose in the mid-day sun –
clothes, purses mindlessly abandoned
on the grass – only my blind
gaze would meet your mind's eye.

If There is an Apocalypse,

I would not attend my high school reunion,
I could not bear all that exhausted smoke.

I'd have a picnic – devouring dry bones,
tasting arid wine in the Valley of the Shadow.

The undead, eyes shut, yet seeing,
would not shudder at my unseeing.

The spirits would speak my name
and return my shuttered gaze,

dancing with me in the night,
twirling with me in the shade.

Sabrina's Song for Uppity

My porcupine, my Turkish Delight,
you jump-started my night into day –
scattering the jigsaw pieces of my self
from Chelsea to the gods' hideaway.

In the beginning, you, dark rainbow,
eclipsed the sun. I dreamed your cane,
a sword, made me run – that I became
salt when I looked your way.

Until your sleight of hand changed
my nightmares into summer's play.
Baking me lasagna, massaging
my headaches away –

walking on Broadway as if you owned
this town – you knocked my terrors
(smack!) onto the ground.

That's All Folks!

Dreaming of angels flying,
bats on a wing
and a prayer at dawn,
I tell the woman downstairs
swatting night terrors
to stop that caterwauling.
If the world does end,
there's nothing
we can do
except, like wobbly,
adventurous ducks,
put on our webbed
feet and glide
into the rising sun.